D1445081

Essential Events

THE TITANIC

BY SUE VANDER HOOK

Essential Events

THE TITANIC

BY SUE VANDER HOOK

Content Consultant
Michael S. Sweeney
Professor of Journalism
Utah State University

ABDO
Publishing Company

CREDITS

Published by ABDO Publishing Company, 8000 West 78th Street, Edina, Minnesota 55439. Copyright © 2008 by Abdo Consulting Group, Inc. International copyrights reserved in all countries. No part of this book may be reproduced in any form without written permission from the publisher. The Essential Library™ is a trademark and logo of ABDO Publishing Company.

Printed in the United States.

Editor: Paula Lewis
Copy Editor: Patricia Stockland
Interior Design and Production: Rebecca Daum
Cover Design: Rebecca Daum

Library of Congress Cataloging-in-Publication Data
Vander Hook, Sue, 1949-
  The Titanic / Sue Vander Hook.
    p. cm. — (Essential events)
  Includes bibliographical references.
  ISBN 978-1-60453-051-3
  1. Titanic (Steamship)—Juvenile literature. 2. Shipwrecks—North Atlantic Ocean—Juvenile literature. I. Title.

  G530.T6V36 2008
  910.9163'4—dc22

                              2007031213

TABLE OF CONTENTS

Passengers in the water and in lifeboats watch as the Titanic *sinks.*

VOICES OF THE ATLANTIC

Seventeen-year-old Jack Thayer had been pulled underwater to an unimaginable depth, and now he was being pushed back up. Finally he surfaced, gasping for air and protecting his head from floating debris. His hand touched an overturned lifeboat. Clinging to it were several exhausted men, also fighting to survive. With one man's help, Jack climbed onto the overturned lifeboat and held on with icy hands. Eventually, 30 people would find their way to this lifeboat, Collapsible B. It was their last hope of survival.

Approximately 50 yards (46 m) away loomed the most magnificent ship in the world—no longer gliding effortlessly and majestically across the ocean. The bow, or front, had broken off and was under water. The stern, or rear, of the gigantic ship rose slowly out of the frigid Atlantic, pointing upward in an unnatural vertical pose.

Jack could see hundreds of people still on the stern of the ship scurrying to reach the highest portion of the deck. Many passengers clung to objects so they would not slide into the sea. Some fell helplessly into the freezing water. Jack heard the groans of crushing steel and the screams of nearly 1,500 people still on this ship called *Titanic*.

In those early morning hours of April 15, 1912, the broken stern

Wrong Side Up

Collapsible B was stored upside down. The crew was unable to launch it upright. It slid into the water upside down. People in the water climbed aboard and balanced on the bottom of the boat. This was extremely precarious, as the boat was in danger of flipping or losing its air bubble and sinking at any time.

slowly began to sink, taking people and wreckage with it. Many people jumped overboard to avoid being crushed by the ship or pulled deep into the water with the sinking ship. The lifeboat Jack was on had been pulled in closer to the disaster, and now three massive propellers were above him.

The lights on the *Titanic* flickered, then turned off one last time. At 2:20 a.m. on Monday, April 15, 1912, the remains of the *Titanic* disappeared into the Atlantic Ocean with approximately 1,200 people still on board.

More people tried to get on the overturned Collapsible B. "We helped them on until we were packed like sardines,"

The Truth About the Titanic

On April 10, 1912, 53-year-old Colonel Archibald Gracie boarded the *Titanic* at Southampton, England, to return home to New York. He had been vacationing in Europe after writing a book, *The Truth About Chickamauga*. The topic of the book was a Civil War battle in which his father had fought.

On board the *Titanic*, Gracie spent his time reading in the library, socializing, and exercising in the heated saltwater swimming pool. On Sunday, April 14, Gracie dined with Clinch Smith and Edward Kent. Later, Gracie enjoyed coffee and the music of the ship's orchestra. He went to bed early so he would be well rested for his exercise sessions in the morning. But at 11:45 p.m., he was awakened by a jolt. After getting dressed, he made his way to the deck, where his friend Smith handed him a piece of ice as a souvenir of the iceberg the ship had just struck.

Gracie survived the sinking of the *Titanic* and wrote another book—*The Truth About the* Titanic.

Jack recalled. "Then out of self-preservation, we had to turn some away."[1] As Harry Senior, a member of the *Titanic* crew, tried to climb onto Collapsible B, he was hit on the head with an oar. Undeterred, he swam to the other side and managed to climb aboard. One more person on the overturned lifeboat, however, might cause it to sink. The men steered the lifeboat away to avoid contact with struggling swimmers. When another man approached, those onboard asked him not to get on. Senior remembered the man politely said, "All right, boys; good luck and God bless you."[2] No one knew who that brave man was.

Others on the lifeboat included Archibald Gracie, a colonel in the U.S. Army and a writer. Charles Lightoller, the second officer of the *Titanic,* made it onto the lifeboat. So did Harold Bride, the assistant wireless telegraph operator who sent distress messages until the ship was nearly under water.

Survivors in the 28° Fahrenheit (-2°C) saltwater begged for a lifeboat to pick them up. Including the

The Victims

Determining the number of victims was not easy. Official lists of passengers and crew do not provide accurate numbers. In some cases, passengers boarded under false names in an attempt to hide their identities. Some of those passengers were counted twice. The ship may also have had unidentified stowaways. Even some of the *Titanic* crew never boarded, and they were counted among the dead.

One of the Last on Board

Before the *Titanic* went under, the chief baker, Charles Joughin, threw deck chairs overboard to be used as flotation devices. He stayed on the ship until the stern nearly disappeared, and then he stepped into the water. He later said, "I do not believe my head went under at all."[3] Joughin was pushed off Collapsible B, but his cook, Isaac Maynard, was able to hold onto him as he floated in the water. Joughin survived.

overturned Collapsible B, there were 20 lifeboats. Most of the lifeboats had rowed as far as possible away from the *Titanic*. Many lifeboats were only half full. Although people could hear the pleas for help, they did not turn back. Some were afraid their lifeboats would overturn if swamped by desperate people. As each minute passed, it became more quiet as passengers and crew members lost their battle with the frigid cold.

By daylight, approximately 700 people had survived the cold night. Approximately 300 frozen bodies in life jackets floated about. Many of the survivors would never talk about that night. Some would testify about the tragedy before the U.S. Senate and the British government. Others, like Jack Thayer and Archibald Gracie, would write down what they remembered.

How could a ship that was called "unsinkable" be swallowed up so quickly and quietly into the depths of the sea?

The Titanic sinking into the Atlantic Ocean

The Titanic *under construction in Belfast, Ireland*

THE MAKING OF A GIANT

he *Titanic* lost its battle with the Atlantic and lay broken on the ocean floor. It became a tomb for those who were forced to go down with it on its 2.5-mile (4-km) plunge. Only five days earlier, on April 10, 1912, the giant ship had been

hailed the biggest and best in the world. It had
won an unofficial competition among shipbuilders
and attracted the wealthiest people as guests for its
maiden voyage.

There was no airplane travel at that time, so the
only way to cross the Atlantic Ocean was by ship. In
the 1800s, space on ships was cramped. Travelers
slept in small rooms often no larger than the bed.
Walkways along the deck were crowded with crates,
chicken coops, and other cargo.

By the early 1900s, however, passenger ships
had more than doubled in size. Some of the newer
ships were similar to lavish hotels. Travel between
Europe and the United States became more
common. Wealthy people were willing to pay for the
costly magnificent first-class accommodations that
matched their lifestyles. Second-class travel aboard
these ships was considered luxurious compared to
the nineteenth-century ships. Even the lowest parts
of the new ships, where third-class passengers stayed,
were simple but comfortable.

Building the Best

Rivalry was fierce among shipbuilders. British,
German, French, and American shipping lines

competed to produce the fastest, biggest, and most splendid ships. In 1906, the British Cunard Line built two huge ships—the *Lusitania* and the *Mauretania*. These ships broke all records for size, weight, and speed. The *Mauretania*, the faster of the two, broke several transatlantic records. It cut the time to cross the Atlantic to less than four-and-a-half days. The two ships rapidly made the Cunard Line the leader in the shipping industry.

However, the British White Star Line was not to be outdone. On a summer evening in 1907, two men met in London to devise a plan to build bigger and better ships. They met at the house of Lord William James Pirrie, head of Harland & Wolff shipbuilders. Pirrie was joined by J. Bruce Ismay, managing director of the White Star Line. That night, the men sketched plans for three nearly identical ships: the *Olympic*, the *Titanic*, and the *Gigantic* (later renamed *Britannic*). If the first two ships were successful, they would build the third.

The owner of the company, American businessman J. Pierpont Morgan, agreed with the plan. This successful banker and investor was eager not only to surpass Cunard but to make hefty profits from the trio of ships as well.

Construction of the *Olympic* began almost immediately. A special dry dock was built in Belfast, Ireland, to accommodate the construction of such an enormous project. When finished, the *Olympic* was the heaviest man-made, movable object of its time. In March 1909, work began on the *Titanic* at an adjacent dock. It would surpass the *Olympic*'s weight by approximately

Were the Rivets Responsible?

The *Titanic*'s hull was constructed of steel plates that were up to 36 feet (11 m) long by 6 feet (1.8 m) wide and 1 inch (2.5 cm) thick. Deck plating on the upper decks was thicker. The plates were attached to the ship's frame in overlapping strips called strakes and then riveted together. Once the rivets were in place, watertight putty was forced into the joints with a high-pressured pump. Workers tested sections of the ship by filling them with water to make sure the joints did not let in any water. Approximately 3 million rivets were used in building the *Titanic*.

When the ship hit the iceberg, the blow caused the heads of the rivets to break off, allowing water to gush in through the joints. Rivets that were recovered from the wreck were found to be made of iron that would be considered substandard today, but met all construction requirements of 1912. Some believe that if the rivets had been made of stronger metal, the deck plates would have held together and water would not have flooded the ship.

1,000 tons (907 t) by weighing in at 46,328 tons (42,028 t). The *Titanic* was also longer than its sister ship by 9 inches (23 cm), measuring 882.75 feet (269.06 m). Each ship was nearly as long as three football fields. Both were longer than the rival ships *Lusitania* and *Mauretania* by approximately 120 feet (37 m).

The *Olympic*, which was completed first, was praised as "the achievement of the age."[1] It set out on June 14, 1911, for a successful maiden voyage from England to New York. Captain Edward J. Smith, who had more than 40 years experience at sea, was at the helm.

Almost one year later, the *Titanic* was finished. On April 2, 1912, at 6:00 a.m., the largest ship in the world moved out of the Belfast shipyard. Captain Smith, now known as the "Millionaire's Captain," was in charge. His crew included Chief Officer Henry Wilde, First Officer

A Successful Career

Captain Edward John Smith was born in Hanley, Stoke-on-Trent, England, on January 27, 1850. At the age of 13, he became an apprentice on the clipper ship *Senator Weber*. In 1887, Smith began working for the White Star Line and commanded his first ship. During his career, he captained 17 White Star ships. Considered the White Star's top seaman, Smith often took the company's ships on their sea trials and maiden voyages. Prior to the *Titanic*'s first voyage, Smith had captained the *Olympic* for almost a year. He planned to retire after the *Titanic*'s maiden voyage.

William Murdoch, and Second Officer Charles
Lightoller.

SAFE AND SEAWORTHY

In the open waters of the Atlantic, the gigantic
ship began its sea trials—speeding up, stopping,
turning at various speeds, and making an emergency
stop. Inspectors tested the wireless radio-telegraph
equipment and examined safety gear and lifeboats.
According to British Board of Trade officials, the
Titanic passed the test. The ship was declared ready for
its maiden voyage.

Six years earlier, aboard White Star Line's
ship the *Adriatic*, Captain Smith boasted, "I cannot
imagine any condition which would cause a ship to
founder [sink]. ... Modern ship-building has gone
beyond that."[2] According to Harland & Wolff, even
in the worst possible accident, the *Titanic* should
stay afloat for two to three days. The lower section
of the ship was designed with 16 compartments.
Each one could be sealed off with an automatic
watertight door in the event of a punctured hull.
The ship was designed to stay afloat if any two of the
compartments flooded. It could even float if the first
four compartments at the bow took on water.

Safety First

The Engelhardt life-boats were named after their developer, Captain Engelhardt. The first model of an Engelhardt collapsible lifeboat was shown at the World's Fair in Paris in 1900. After this, the Engelhardt Collapsible Life Boat Co. was founded, and the invention was patented in several countries.

These lifeboats had wooden bottoms that were surrounded by cork. Collapsible canvas sides could be lifted and put into place quickly either on deck or in the water. When the sides were down, the boats essentially laid flat and could be stored neatly on the top deck. They did not take up as much room as regular lifeboats and held more people.

Each of the *Titanic*'s 16 davits, or lifeboat cranes, was capable of lowering three lifeboats. The *Titanic* could have accommodated up to 48 lifeboats. However, that number was slashed to 32 and then to 16 when complaints arose that the boats would block the ocean view. Four collapsible lifeboats, called Engelhardts, were also on the ship, stored upside down. In all, there were 20 lifeboats—Lifeboats 1 through 16 and Collapsibles A through D. If completely filled, the lifeboats could hold 1,176 people, just more than half of the passengers and crew members. But lifeboats did not seem very important to anyone. After all, the ship was considered safe from all disasters. It was thought to be unsinkable.

Titanic *lifeboats and the davits that lowered the lifeboats into the water*

The Titanic *was approximately four city blocks long.*

MAIDEN VOYAGE

hen the *Titanic*'s sea trials were completed, the crew prepared to leave Belfast. At 8:00 p.m. on April 2, 1912, the *Titanic* set out for Southampton, a major port on the south side of England. In addition to a small crew, Thomas

Andrews, managing director of Harland & Wolff, was on board. He had supervised every detail of the *Titanic*'s construction. Now he was enjoying the first voyage of his great accomplishment.

Crowds of spectators came to celebrate the *Titanic*'s arrival at Southampton. For seven days, the impressive ship berthed at a new dock made especially for the *Titanic* and the *Olympic*. Observers and reporters gathered at the dock to catch a glimpse of this maritime marvel. With nine decks, it was as tall as an 11-story building. Including the four funnels, the ship towered 25 stories. The funnels rose 60 feet (18 m) above the top deck. Three of the funnels would belch steam and smoke created by the massive coal-fed boilers that powered the steam engines. The fourth funnel was added for appearance to equal the number of funnels on the *Lusitania* and the *Mauretania*. Passengers and spectators admired the ship's black steel exterior and windows instead of portholes. The first promenade, or walkway, was enclosed with glass so passengers would not be bothered by ocean spray.

In New York, on the other side of the Atlantic, people eagerly anticipated the arrival of the *Titanic* on April 17.

Preparing for the Guests

On Wednesday morning, April 10, 1912, it was time for final preparations for the *Titanic's* voyage. Just past dawn, 891 workers began boarding the ship. Some gathered at the lifeboats to perform a 30-minute drill. Eighteen crew members in two lifeboats were lowered over the side to row around to ensure the lifeboats were in good working order.

Meanwhile, the rest of the ship was abuzz with preparations. Freight had to be loaded—tea, lace, silk, wine, books, window frames, ostrich feathers, and an automobile. Cooks and bakers organized 36,000 apples, 1,000 pounds (454 kg) of grapes, 1,500 gallons (5,676 L) of milk, and 1,000 bottles of wine. The dinnerware included 12,000 dinner plates, 4,500 soup bowls, 29,000 glasses, and 2,000 saltshakers—all custom designed for the White Star Line.

The 390 stewards and stewardesses busily arranged 7,500 bath towels and 18,000 bed sheets. Their duties included making beds, cleaning cabins, and putting away clothes. They would also deliver meals and run errands. Nine men were assigned to shine shoes of first-class passengers. Other crew members included barbers, a carpenter, a night watchman, a window cleaner, a masseuse, an exercise instructor, and a squash coach. There were also bath attendants, bartenders, florists, and two wireless radio operators. Five postal clerks were on board this luxury ship that also transported mail.

Other members of the crew included six lookouts. Two lookouts at a time kept two-hour shifts in the crow's nest, a boxlike perch on the main mast near the bow of the ship. The lookouts were to watch for approaching hazards in the water. In the lowest depths of the ship, 340 men worked as engineers, electricians, greasers, boilermakers, and firemen. Coal was continually shoveled into huge furnaces that powered the engines.

At 9:30 a.m. on April 10, 1912, J. Bruce Ismay boarded the ship to make a final inspection. The maiden voyage of the *Titanic* was one trip he would not miss.

BOARDING PASSENGERS AT SOUTHAMPTON

About the time Ismay boarded, a charter boat train arrived from Waterloo Station in London. It

RMS *Titanic*

In addition to passenger service, the shipping lines also made money transporting small cargo and mail on their transatlantic excursions. British ships that carried England's mail displayed the letters RMS (Royal Mail Steamship) before their name.

brought more than 200 second-class and nearly 500 third-class passengers to the *Titanic*. Ticket-holding travelers began boarding the ship. Visitors and reporters were welcomed aboard to tour and explore the *Titanic* before it launched. For more than two hours, people strolled along the decks or browsed through the library. Some just enjoyed walking along the promenade, mingling and listening to the ship's orchestra play festive ragtime tunes.

The atmosphere was joyous. People were amazed at the elegance. One second-class passenger, former schoolteacher Lawrence Beesley, wandered into the gym with two friends who had come to see him off. As they were trying out the stationary bicycles, two photographers from a popular London newspaper came in. They wanted pictures of the equipment in action. Beesley later wrote:

> one passenger on the electric "horse," another on the "camel," while the laughing group of onlookers watched the inexperienced riders vigorously shaken up and down as he controlled the little motor which made the machines imitate so realistically horse and camel exercise.[1]

At 11:30 a.m., a boat with lush blue upholstery and gold braid arrived from London. Many of *Titanic*'s first-class passengers were on board. Of the 324 first-class passengers, 171 boarded at Southampton.

These passengers included millionaire Isidor Straus, owner of Macy's department store and a former New York state congressman. Straus, his wife Ida, her maid, and Straus's manservant were returning to New York after vacationing on the French Riviera. Colonel Archibald Gracie would spend time socializing, discussing the Civil War with Straus, and exercising in the gym. Major Archibald Butt was a military aide to President William Howard Taft and former President Theodore Roosevelt. British-born W.T. Stead was on his way to the United States to take part in a peace conference at the request of President Taft.

Almost all of the 285 second-class passengers boarded at Southampton. They came from all walks of life—

The Orchestra

The White Star Line also provided entertainment. Wallace Henry Hartley, an accomplished violinist, was the ship's bandmaster. A three-member orchestra played for second-class passengers in their own dining room and deck. A five-member orchestra performed for first-class travelers. The musicians played for teatime, after-dinner concerts, and Sunday church services.

All eight members of *Titanic*'s orchestras perished with the ship. A plaque in their honor was unveiled at Liverpool's Philharmonic Hall in England on November 4, 1912. Ironically, the plaque survived when the hall was destroyed by fire in 1933. The plaque was placed in a new hall that opened six years later. In the 1940s, both the plaque and the building survived heavy bombing during World War II even as nearby buildings were destroyed.

Passengers stroll on the deck of the Titanic.

miners, bricklayers, painters, ministers, servants, farmers, carpenters, and teachers. Some traveled as families; others traveled alone. Percy Andrew Bailey, 18, was traveling by himself on his way to Akron, Ohio, to begin an apprenticeship as a butcher. On board, he wrote a letter to his parents:

> The Titanic *is a marvel I can tell you I have never seen such a sight in all my life, she is like a floating palace, everything up to date.*[2]

Passengers came from all over the world. They spoke English, French, Italian, Chinese, Swedish, Dutch, Russian, and other languages. Nine-week-old Millvina Dean boarded with her parents and older brother Bertram. They were emigrating from England to Wichita, Kansas, where her father hoped to open a tobacco shop. The Asplund family was returning to the United States after spending time in Sweden. Five-year-old Lillian Gertrud Asplund was their only daughter. She had a twin brother, two older brothers, and a three-year-old brother.

At the last minute, passengers from other ships were transferred to the *Titanic*. A local coal workers' strike had reduced the coal supply in England. Coal was transferred to the *Titanic* from smaller ships whose voyages were then canceled. The *Titanic* was sure to have enough fuel to power its engines and there was plenty of room for more passengers.

By the end of the morning, all travelers were on board, and all visitors had left the ship. The *Titanic* was ready to launch. One visitor commented:

None of us had the slightest fear for her safety, she was the last word in modern efficiency and was said to be literally unsinkable.[3]

Three whistles blew at 12:15 p.m., signaling the *Titanic*'s departure. As tugboats helped it out from the dock, crowds cheered and threw flowers in the water as they waved good-bye to friends and family. Five minutes later, the *Titanic* nearly collided with the *New York*, a nearby ship moored at the dock. The suction and wave caused by the *Titanic*'s huge propellers had caused the *New York*'s thick ropes to strain and break, sending its gangway crashing into the water and moving the ship toward the *Titanic*.

Passenger Edward Pomeroy Colley wrote a letter to his cousin about the mishap:

We nearly had a collision to start with coming out of Southampton. We passed close to a ship … and the suction of our ship drew her out into the stream, and

Young Survivors

The youngest passenger on the *Titanic,* nine-week-old Millvina Dean, boarded the ship with her parents in Southampton. She survived the ordeal and was rescued on Lifeboat 10 with her mother and brother. Her father died in the disaster. Millvina was eight years old before she learned that she had been on the *Titanic*. In 1996, at the age of 84, she traveled to Belfast as guest of honor at the Titanic Historical Society convention.

The Asplund family also boarded the *Titanic* at Southampton. Five-year-old Lillian, her mother, and three-year-old brother Felix were rescued on Lifeboat 15. Their mother, Selma Asplund, died on April 15, 1964, the fifty-second anniversary of the *Titanic* tragedy that took the lives of four members of her family. Felix died at the age of 73. Lillian lived to be 99. She was the last survivor to have memories of the disaster. Throughout her life, she refused to talk about the tragedy.

snapped the bonds that held her, and round she swung across our bows! She had no steam up; so had to be pulled back by tugs, and we had to reverse.[4]

Due to quick action by Captain Smith and the harbor pilot, the ships did not collide, but some people thought it was a bad omen. Others quickly forgot about the near mishap and went about enjoying the fine features of the ship.

Boarding Passengers at Cherbourg

Approximately five hours later, after a peaceful crossing of the English Channel, the *Titanic* arrived at Cherbourg, France. No dock was large enough for the *Titanic*, so passengers were ferried to it.

Some of the wealthiest people in the world boarded at Cherbourg. John B. Thayer, a vice president of the Pennsylvania Railroad, boarded with his wife, Marian, and son, Jack. Millionaire George Widener, from Philadelphia, Pennsylvania, came aboard with his wife and 27-year-old son, Harry. Walter Douglas, 50, was the son of the man who started Quaker Oats and had amassed a fortune of $4 million. Douglas boarded with his wife, Mahala, and her maid.

The wealthiest passenger was John Jacob Astor. He came from a wealthy family, but he had also made his own fortune in real estate. His personal fortune was estimated at $100 million. Two-and-a-half years earlier, 47-year-old Astor had caused a scandal when he divorced his wife. The scandal grew when he married 18-year-old Madeleine Force in September 1911. To escape social pressure, the couple had left New York for a vacation in Paris and Egypt. Now Astor and his wife, who was five months pregnant, were returning home. With them were Astor's manservant and Madeleine's maid and private nurse.

Lady Duff Gordon and her husband Sir Cosmo Duff Gordon were among the elite. Lady Duff was the owner of one of the great fashion design houses, with locations in London, New York City, Paris, and Chicago. Her clients included the Duchess of York, who later became England's Queen Mary. One passenger—millionaire Margaret Tobin Brown—had already made an impact on the world through her involvement with the Women's Suffrage Association. Her work encouraged literacy, education, suffrage, and human rights.

Benjamin Guggenheim traveled with a French singer named Madame Léontine Aubart. They

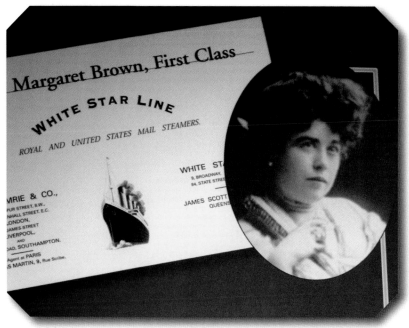

A photograph of passenger Margaret Brown and a reproduction of her boarding pass

were accompanied by a valet, chauffeur, and Aubart's maid. Guggenheim had inherited his immense wealth from his father, a prosperous mining industrialist. But he was also a successful businessman in his own right.

ON TO IRELAND

The ship left Cherbourg later that day and headed for Ireland. At about noon the next day, the *Titanic* dropped anchor at Queenstown (now

Cobh) on the south shore of Ireland. Queenstown did not have a dock large enough for the *Titanic*, so the ship was anchored approximately 2 miles (3 km) from shore. Two boats, called tenders, brought passengers, cargo, and mailbags out to the ship. The tenders also took eight passengers and one crew member back to shore. They had no idea how fortunate they were that their journey on the *Titanic* ended at Queenstown.

At 1:30 p.m. on Thursday, April 11, 1912, the *Titanic* steamed away from Ireland and headed for New York. It was a beautiful clear spring day. The ocean was exceptionally calm. Journalist W.T. Stead wrote to his wife that the *Titanic* was as firm as a rock in the sea. Travel over the next four days would be smooth, and the passengers would bask in extravagance, good food, and entertainment. ⌐

In the shipyard, a group of workers stand by the Titanic's propellers.

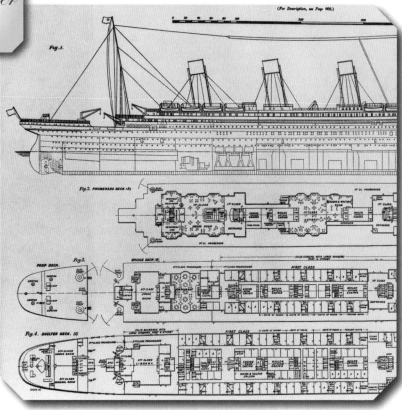

Deck plans of the Titanic

Four Days of
Extravagance

he *Titanic* had nine decks—ten including the
very lowest level of the ship, called the belly
or the Tank Top. Cargo and coal reserves were stored
in the belly. The ship's 29 gigantic round boilers,
containing 162 furnaces, spanned upward two more

decks and heated water to produce steam for the engines. Stokers endlessly shoveled coal into the furnaces.

Above the Tank Top was the Orlop Deck, where the ship's three anchors were stored. The Orlop Deck also stored cargo, including 3,364 sacks of mail and a passenger's Renault automobile. Electrical rooms routed electricity to power lights, heaters, refrigeration, the wireless telegraph equipment, and, if necessary, to activate the watertight doors. Electric elevators carried first- and second-class passengers from one deck to another. Other space was taken up with storage rooms for groceries, wine, champagne, and mineral water. Ample refrigerated storage space contained meat, cheese, butter, milk, eggs, and even ice cream.

A Tour of the Passenger Decks

The seven decks above the Orlop Deck were named A through G. The lowest level with passenger accommodations was G Deck. It included dormitory-style sleeping areas for the crew and third-class passengers. The cabins had foldaway beds, wash basins with running water, and electric lighting—quite luxurious compared to other ships.

The aft section of G Deck included second-class passenger cabins that slept two to four people in bunks and sofa beds. With mahogany furniture, linoleum floors, and electric lighting, these second-class berths were as nice as first-class accommodations on many other ships. Since bathrooms were not provided on G Deck, passengers used the facilities on the F and E decks.

G Deck also included the squash court, reserved for first-class passengers only. It also housed the post office, where clerks sorted letters and packages.

On the next deck up, F Deck, spectators could watch a squash tournament from a gallery above the open court. This deck housed engineers, stewards, cooks, butchers, bakers, the postal workers, and some second- and third-class passengers.

Hearty food was served on F Deck in the third-class dining room, which could hold 470 people. Meals were included in the price of a third-class one-way ticket. Typically, a third-class breakfast included porridge, beef, potatoes, bread and butter, plum pudding, and tea or coffee. The midday meal was most likely roast beef with potatoes. People could request fish instead of beef, and kosher food was available for Jewish passengers. Dinner in the early evening, called tea, offered a main dish, cheese, and biscuits. Supper later in the evening consisted of gruel, cheese, and biscuits.

F Deck included one of the most unique features of the *Titanic*—a swimming pool. The *Olympic* was the only other ship with a pool. The *Titanic*'s heated saltwater pool was restricted to first-class passengers. Two showers and changing rooms were provided. Portholes on one side allowed natural sunlight to pour in on the swimmers. The pool was available at separate designated times for men and women.

E Deck, one level up, included carefully separated cabins for three

A Post Office at Sea

The *Titanic*'s five mail clerks—three Americans and two British—boarded at Southampton, England. They were not employed by the White Star Line, but they were representatives of the New York and Southampton branches of the sea post office.

Directly below the well-organized mail room was a mail storage area. A safe compartment stored approximately 200 sacks of registered mail. During the course of the journey, the mail clerks were expected to sort approximately 400,000 letters before the ship arrived in New York. In addition, the mail clerks sorted the many letters and postcards written by *Titanic* passengers as they traveled.

When the ship struck the iceberg, the mail clerks were celebrating mail clerk Oscar Woody's forty-fourth birthday, which fell on the following day, April 15, 1912. As the ship sank, the mail clerks worked endlessly to bring mail sacks out of the rising waters to higher decks. None of the mail clerks survived the disaster. Two of their bodies were recovered and buried at sea.

Lifeboat Regulations

The *Titanic* provided 16 wooden lifeboats and 4 collapsible Engelhardt lifeboats. If filled to capacity, these lifeboats would have held less than half of the passengers and crew. This surpassed the requirements of the British Board of Trade.

classes of passengers. The passengers in the first-class cabins kept crew members, also housed on this level, busy. First-class passengers only had to ring a bell inside their cabins for a steward to come to see what they needed. Second- and first-class passengers on E Deck could reach the upper decks by elevators. Third-class passengers used the stairways.

The elaborate Grand Staircase extended from D Deck up to the Boat Deck, which was above A Deck. At the bottom of the Grand Staircase, on D Deck, an elegant reception area spanned the width of the ship for first-class passengers to relax and socialize before dinner. Revolving doors led into the dining room, the largest public area on the ship. A stunning room with oak furnishings, large windows, and a glass dome top, it could seat approximately 550 people. Recessed areas were available for private dining.

The center of the reception area included a dance floor with a raised stage for the orchestra. The galley where food was prepared was located at one end. It contained the two largest stoves in the world as well as nineteen ovens, four grills, two large roasters, and steam ovens. The ship had its own bakery and butcher shop. The first-class pantry stored the finest in china, silver, and glass. Meals were included in first-class tickets.

Further aft from this grand room was the second-class dining room that spanned the width of the ship. Diners sat at long tables in comfortable swivel chairs. Next door was a second-class public room. The tapestry-covered furniture made it an attractive place for passengers to chat and relax before meals. Although the food in second-class dining was not as elegant as first class, the six-course meals were of fine quality. Meals were also included in the price of a second-class one-way ticket.

The office of Chief Purser McElroy was on C Deck near the Grand Staircase. The ship encouraged its passengers to deposit their most valuable items with the purser, who kept them in a locked safe until the ship docked. Passengers could also stop by the office to purchase tickets for the swimming pool, the steam baths, and other facilities. They could request telegrams to be sent to people on shore or aboard passing ships. The purser would write down the message and send it to the Marconi Room on the uppermost deck, where wireless operators Jack Phillips and Harold Bride sent out and received messages all day and evening.

C Deck, and all decks above it, housed only first-class passengers. Most of the rooms were suites with two bedrooms and a private bath. A larger suite, or stateroom, included a bedroom, drawing room, sitting room, private bath, and sometimes a private dining room. The rooms were decorated lavishly in styles such as Italian Renaissance, Louis XV, or Queen Anne.

People could walk along the first-class promenade and socialize or relax on reclining deck chairs. Near the stern, separated from first class, a second-class promenade was enclosed with a long row of large windows. The second-class library was also on C Deck. Its wood-paneled walls, mahogany furniture, tall bookcase, and large windows covered with silk drapes made it a peaceful place to read and write.

Dinner Is Served

Food for the first-class dining room was prepared on D Deck in the same kitchen as second-class meals. The last dinner served in first class consisted of 11 courses, including canapés, oysters, soup, poached salmon, filet mignon, chicken, lamb, duck, roast beef, potatoes, carrots, peas, rice, and roasted squab. Also served were asparagus salad, chocolate éclairs, peaches, and cheeses. One of the most interesting dishes was Waldorf Pudding, a sweet item served with the tenth course.

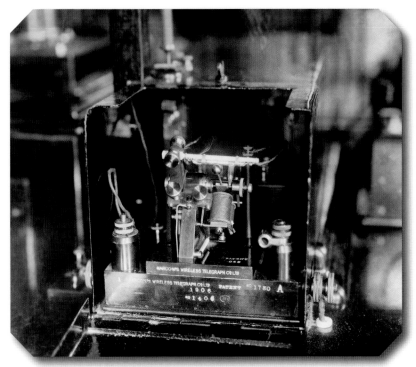

This Marconi wireless was on the Carpathia *and is similar to the* Titanic*'s wireless.*

The most expensive rooms on the ship were the two parlor suites on B Deck. Each suite had two bedrooms, a sitting room, a private bathroom, two walk-in closets, and a private enclosed promenade deck with windows that looked out over the ocean. There was also a separate cabin for a servant. One of these suites was occupied by Charlotte Cardeza and her son Thomas from Germantown, Pennsylvania.

A Personal Maid

Mrs. Charlotte Cardeza's maid, Anna Ward, was responsible for 14 trunks, 4 suitcases, and 3 crates of baggage. Mrs. Cardeza's wardrobe included 70 dresses, 38 feather boas, and 10 fur coats.

The other parlor suite was occupied by J. Bruce Ismay, his secretary, and manservant. The suite was designed by and originally reserved for J. Pierpont Morgan. But at the last minute, Morgan canceled his trip on the *Titanic*.

B Deck was also home to the Á la Carte Restaurant, where passengers could order food and drinks anytime between 8:00 a.m. and 11:00 p.m. The younger first-class passengers often met at the Café Parisien for meals and to socialize. Beyond the restaurant, a smoking room with carved oak walls and oak furniture was available to second-class passengers. At the stern was the Poop Deck, a rounded deck that housed equipment and also served as a third-class promenade.

The top of the Grand Staircase overlooked A Deck, also called the Promenade Deck. This deck was covered overhead by the Boat Deck, but it had an unobstructed view of the sea. The front part of the walk at the bow of the ship included windows that could be closed in bad weather or if the sea spray was bothersome. One large first-class cabin on that

The first-class reading room

level was occupied by Thomas Andrews of Harland & Wolff—the *Titanic*'s shipbuilders.

The first-class reading room, furnished with comfortable armchairs and tables for writing, was also on A Deck. This room was frequented mostly by women. Next to it was a lounge illuminated by wall lights, gigantic mirrors, and an elaborate light in the center. A large fireplace was at one end. Passengers could relax in comfortable chairs or play cards.

Nearby, in the smoking room, men could socialize at the ornate bar or sit by the large fireplace in heavy leather chairs.

The beautifully crafted oak and wrought iron Grand Staircase ended at the top of A Deck. The staircase was similar on each deck with a middle handrail that supported a bronze cherub holding a lamp in one hand. The top deck, however, included a massive glass dome that let sunlight in during the day and glowed with electric lights at night. On the landing just below the dome was an ornate clock surrounded by two figures that represented the crowning of time with honor and glory.

The stairs exited near the gymnasium on the Boat Deck—the top level of the ship. Along each side of the deck hung 16 lifeboats on davits that were used to launch the lifeboats off the side of the ship. Each lifeboat was covered with canvas to keep it dry. The four collapsible lifeboats were stored on the roof of the officers' quarters.

Although most of this deck was used for boats, offices, and equipment, there was still room for people to walk. The view of the ocean was magnificent—due to a drastic reduction in the number of lifeboats that hung on each side.

A re-creation of a portion of the Grand Staircase

Chief Purser McElroy and Captain Smith

FIELDS OF ICE

y noon on Friday, April 12, 1912, the *Titanic* had traveled 386 miles (621 km). Under the watch of Captain Smith, the *Titanic* was making good time and increasing its speed daily. The sea was so calm that passengers hardly noticed the ship was moving. They leisurely strolled along the decks and played cards in the lounges. Some listened to the orchestra or snacked at the Café Parisien. Lawrence Beesley later remembered:

> The sea was calm ... but often rather cold, generally too cold to sit out on deck to read or write, so that many of us spent a good part of the time in the library, reading and writing.[1]

On the lower levels, third-class passengers danced to Irish music provided by a pipe and fiddle or a bagpipe and piano. Others played ball on deck.

In spite of a fire in one of the coal rooms, nothing was out of the ordinary. No one considered it cause for alarm when the French ship *La Touraine* telegraphed at 7:00 p.m. that it had just passed through a thick ice field. Warnings about ice were not unusual at this time of year. Each

Fighting a Fire

Nearly two weeks after the *Titanic* sank, fireman John Dilley told a reporter from the *Stevens Point* (Wisconsin) *Journal* how flames broke out in one of the *Titanic*'s coal rooms after the ship left Southampton, England. Dilley and 11 other men fought the fire. The passengers knew nothing about it.

The men fought the flames from the day the ship launched until shortly before it struck the iceberg. Only the ocean could put out the flames.

spring, when the weather turned warmer, thousands of large chunks of ice broke away from Greenland's Arctic ice shelf. As the chunks moved south, they melted slowly and broke up into fields of smaller ice. A few hundred large icebergs normally made it as far south as the *Titanic*'s route. But in 1912, an unusually large number had made it farther. A mild winter and spring may have caused more ice to break away earlier in the year. Over the next two days, other ships sent similar warnings to the *Titanic*.

Most passengers were unaware of the warnings, and the crew did not feel it was necessary to tell them. Travelers continued to discover the fine amenities the ship had to offer and pampered themselves with extravagance.

Saturday, April 13, was a beautiful day at sea. By midday, the ship had traveled another 519 miles (835 km), a good distance at an excellent speed. That night, the *Titanic* received another message, this one by signal lamp from the steamer *Rappahannock*, warning of a huge field of ice. Icebergs had drifted farther south than they had in 50 years, jamming ocean routes that were normally passable. Many ships, including the Cunard Line's *Carmania*, encountered dangerous fields of ice.

In spite of multiple warnings, the *Titanic* kept its course and increased its speed. Each day, Captain Smith ordered more engine power and more speed. At 11:00 p.m. on Saturday, warnings stopped coming in because the ship's wireless telegraph system broke down. Wireless operators Phillips and

Bride stayed up all night fixing it. By 5:00 a.m. on Sunday, it was working again. The operators were now very tired and very behind. They scrambled to send passengers' personal telegrams to keep everyone happy.

By noon on Sunday, the *Titanic* had covered an additional 546 miles (879 km), more than either of

When Speed Matters

The Blue Ribband is an award held by a ship that holds the speed record for a transatlantic crossing. Shipping companies created the contest in the 1860s to create publicity for the fastest ship. There were two awards—one for the fastest eastbound crossing and one for the fastest trip westward. The winning ships won the honor to fly a blue pennant from their topmasts.

The Cunard Line's *Mauretania* won the contest in 1909 and retained the record until 1929. In 1935, Sir Harold Keates Hales, a British politician and owner of Hales Brothers shipping company, came up with the idea for a trophy. The Hales Trophy, as it was called, was awarded to the ship with the highest average speed. Traditionally, routes considered for the transatlantic record included New York City as either the point of departure or the destination. Other ships that have won the coveted award are:

- 1938: *Queen Mary*
- 1952: *United States*
- 1998: *Master Cat*

the two previous days. The ocean was still unusually
calm; they were making excellent time. Colonel
Gracie called it a "sea of glass."[2] Captain Smith
predicted an early arrival in New York. He planned
to fire up all the boilers in the engine room and
gradually increase the speed. He hoped the ship
would arrive in New York well ahead of the
scheduled time.

Some believed that Smith, Ismay, and others with
the White Star Line had planned all along to go for
a speed record. Perhaps the *Titanic* could take away
the coveted Blue Ribband award from the *Mauretania*,
which had broken all previous speed records. ⁓

A reenactment of a wireless room

A depiction of the Titanic *hitting an iceberg*

"Iceberg Right Ahead"

Sunday morning, April 14, 1912, was clear and chilly. Some people braved the low temperatures and took early walks on deck before breakfast. Others started the day with exercise. Colonel Gracie had been socializing more than exercising on the cruise, but Sunday morning was different. He wrote:

> *I considered it high time to begin my customary exercises, and determined for the rest of the voyage to patronize the squash racquet court, the gymnasium, the swimming pool, etc.* [1]

Before breakfast, Colonel Gracie met instructor Frederick Wright for a game of squash. After a swim in the pool, Colonel Gracie told both Wright and the pool attendant that he would see them again on Monday morning. He also made an appointment with the gym instructor. He would never keep those appointments.

After breakfast, Colonel Gracie joined other passengers at the 10:30 a.m. church service. In the first-class dining room, Captain Smith read from the ship's prayer book. The five-man orchestra led the congregation in the singing of hymns. They sang the Navy Hymn, which ended, "Oh, hear us when we cry to Thee, for those in peril on the sea!"[2]

By the time lunch was over, the weather had turned much colder. Passengers headed indoors to listen to the orchestra, read in the library, or visit. For unknown reasons, Captain Smith cancelled a lifeboat drill scheduled for 11:30 that morning.

Boat drills and inspections were not a legal requirement.

TELEGRAPH MESSAGES AND REPORTS

Most areas of the ship were quiet, but it was not so peaceful in the Marconi Room. Wireless operators Phillips and Bride were still trying to catch up with a backlog of incoming and outgoing telegrams. Passengers had paid for each telegram request—they expected it to be sent. But telegraph messages from other ships continued to interrupt the operators. The *Caronia* reported ice fields, icebergs, and growlers (smaller icebergs) just north of the *Titanic*'s route. Captain Smith posted the warning for all his officers to see. At 11:40 a.m., the *Noordam* sent a similar warning: "Much ice."[3]

Another report came in at 1:42 p.m. from the White Star liner *Baltic*. It cautioned about icebergs and large quantities of field ice close

Wireless Communication

Guglielmo Marconi (1874–1937), an Italian inventor, is best known for his radiotelegraph system that could transmit over water. Radio stations were built on both sides of the Atlantic Ocean in order to communicate by Morse code with ships at sea. A transatlantic radiotelegraph service was established in 1907, although communication was unreliable.

Phillips and Bride, the Marconi operators on board the *Titanic*, were employed by the Marconi International Marine Communication Company, not the White Star Line. After the sinking of the *Titanic*, Marconi testified regarding the telegraph system and procedures for emergencies at sea.

to the *Titanic*. Captain Smith gave this message to Ismay, who pocketed the paper. Later, Ismay casually showed it to a number of passengers. Seventeen-year-old Jack Thayer was with his parents when Ismay showed them the warning. Thayer recalled:

> *I remember Mr. Ismay showing us a wire regarding the presence of ice and remarking that we would not reach that position until around nine p.m.*[4]

One guest asked Ismay if he was going to slow the ship down. "On the contrary," he said, "we are going to let her run a great deal faster and get out of it."[5]

Soon after the *Baltic*'s message, an iceberg warning from the U.S. Navy was broadcast to all ships in the North Atlantic. That message never made it out of the *Titanic*'s Marconi Room. At 1:45 p.m., another warning came from the German ship *Amerika*.

Outside, the temperature tumbled to 33° Fahrenheit (.6°C). Second Officer Lightoller ordered the ship's carpenter to make sure the fresh water supply was not in danger of freezing. Captain Smith tracked down Ismay and asked him to return the telegram.

Phillips and Bride were still working nonstop to catch up with the stack of telegram requests.

They continued to receive ice warnings. At 7:30 p.m., they intercepted a message from the nearby *Californian* that was meant for another ship. The message reported that three large icebergs were sighted a few miles south of the *Californian*—which was 19 miles (31 km) north of the *Titanic*'s route. Captain Smith was not told about this telegram. He was at a dinner party given is his honor. Ismay was also there, boasting that the ship would no doubt set a speed record.

After dinner, passengers enjoyed the music of the orchestra. In the smoking room, some of the most well-known men on the ship— Colonel Gracie, George Widener,

Ignoring a Warning

The *Californian* was a British steamship designed to transport cotton. It could also carry up to 47 passengers and 55 crew members. On April 5, 1912, the *Californian* left London, England, for Boston, Massachusetts. No passengers were on board.

At 7:30 p.m. on the night of April 14, the *Californian*'s only wireless operator, Cyril Evans, reported three large icebergs a few miles south of the *Californian*. At 10:21 p.m., with the *Californian* in the middle of a large ice field, Captain Stanley Lord stopped the ship for the night. Shortly before 11:00 p.m., *Californian* crew members spotted another ship on the horizon. The captain asked Evans what ships were nearby, to which Evans replied that the *Titanic* was the only ship close to them. Evans was directed to send a message to the *Titanic* that the *Californian* was stopped in ice. After the message was sent, the *Titanic* answered, "Shut up! I am busy."[6] At 11:30 p.m., Evans shut down the wireless system and went to bed. The *Titanic* struck an iceberg ten minutes later.

John Thayer, Major Butt, and artist Francis Millet—discussed politics and business. In the second-class dining room, Reverend E. C. Carter led hundreds of passengers in a religious hymn sing. Third-class passengers socialized in the lower levels of the ship. Thomas Andrews spent the evening in his cabin, writing down changes that should be made to the *Titanic*. Although he thought there were too many screws in the stateroom hat racks, overall he believed the ship was "as nearly perfect as human brains can make her."[7]

Watching for Icebergs

Shortly before 9:00 p.m., Captain Smith stopped by the bridge and told Second Officer Lightoller to notify him if the weather became hazy. A half-hour later, Smith retired to his cabin. About that time, a message arrived from the *Mesaba*. The crew had seen heavy packed ice, field ice, and many large icebergs. Phillips was working the telegraph alone while Bride got some much-needed sleep in the next room. Phillips put the message down with plans to deliver it later. He still had not caught up with the backlog of passenger requests.

By 10:30 p.m., the temperature had dropped below freezing. There was no moon that night, but an array of brilliant stars lit up the sky. The only thing that disturbed the calm night was the black smoke that bellowed out of the forward three funnels. The *Titanic* glided rapidly along at 22 knots per hour (40 km/h).

The deck was nearly deserted. Two lookouts were perched in the crow's nest, watching for icebergs. Usually, lookouts used binoculars, but on this voyage, none were available—they had been forgotten during the last-minute preparations for sailing. Frederick Fleet and Reginald Lee, who started their two-hour duty at 10:00 p.m., strained their eyes looking for splashing water or foam lapping against the rim of an iceberg. But on that night, the water was too calm for splashing.

Lookouts could sometimes smell the strange, clammy odor of ice in the area. One lookout on the previous shift had told Fleet and Lee, "By the smell of it, there is ice about."[8] If the lookouts had been able to see what was ahead of them that night, they would have caught sight of a crowded tangle of icebergs similar to a mountain range. They would have spotted one that rose 100 feet (30 m) above the water. But the danger usually was not in the ice a person could see—it lay in the massive jagged chunk of ice under the water that was approximately eight to ten times larger.

At 11:00 p.m., another telegram arrived. Cyril Evans, the only wireless operator on the *Californian*, said his ship was stopped and surrounded by ice. Phillips responded, "Shut up! I am busy." The numerous interruptions were annoying him as he tried to catch up with his work. Evans stayed at his receiver on the *Californian* for a short while before turning off the system and going to bed. At that time, ships were not required to run their wireless systems 24 hours a day.

For the next 40 minutes, as the *Titanic* lights were turned down, more passengers went to their cabins. Only a few people still socialized in quiet areas of the ship. At 11:40 p.m., however, the calm atmosphere

Tip of the Iceberg

Experienced sailors say they can hear and smell icebergs at night or in foggy conditions. One sailor compared the odor to that of cucumbers.

Icebergs are frozen freshwater ice that originate from glaciers. In northern areas, glaciers flow into the sea and then break apart in a process called calving. Large pieces of ice that float away from calving glaciers are icebergs. All icebergs in the North Atlantic Ocean come from Greenland glaciers. They can float far south before melting.

Only about one-eighth of an iceberg is visible above the water. The remainder of the glacier is under the water and presents a great hazard to ships.

suddenly changed when Fleet spotted a tall, dark mass directly in front of the ship. An iceberg that rose into the sky like a mammoth mountain loomed approximately 500 yards (457 m) ahead. The lookout desperately rang the warning bell three times and shouted into the telephone to the officers on the bridge, "Iceberg right ahead!"[9]

Immediately, First Officer William Murdoch shouted orders to reverse the engines, turn hard to port, and shut the 15 watertight doors. Lee, one of the lookouts, would later testify before a British inquiry:

> it seemed almost as if she might clear it, but I suppose there was ice under water. … It was a dark mass that came through that haze and there was no white appearing until it was just close alongside the ship, and that was just a fringe at the top. … As she struck … there was a certain amount of ice that came on board the ship.[10]

Incorrect Information

The position given by the *Titanic*'s wireless operator was wrong. The location was proved inaccurate 73 years later when the wreck was discovered 13 nautical miles (24 km) to the east and slightly south of the position given. The difference between the two locations was the result of the *Titanic*'s navigators making a small error in fixing its longitude. This was compounded by the ship drifting for more than two hours after it hit the iceberg.

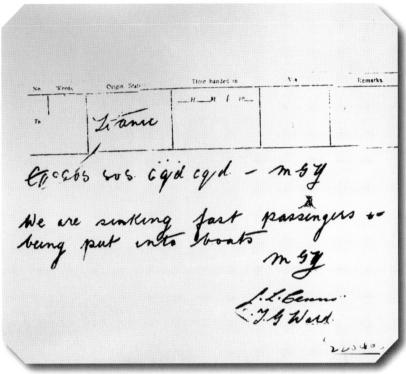

The last radio message sent from the Titanic

The *Titanic* burst onto the airwaves at 12:15 a.m. with a distress call. Ten minutes later, wireless operator Jack Phillips sent this message:

> *We have struck iceberg sinking fast come to our assistance. Position Lat. 41° 46' N., Long. 50° 14' W.*[11]

The message was received by the Russian steamer *Birma*, whose captain turned his vessel and headed full speed toward *Titanic*'s position. But Phillips was not encouraged. The *Birma*, which was 100 miles (161 km) away, estimated its time of arrival at 6:30 a.m. That would be too late for the *Titanic*. Better news came when Phillips learned another ship, the *Carpathia,* was only 58 miles (93 km) away. ⌐

This drawing shows the decks of the Titanic and suggests points of impact
with the iceberg below the waterline.

Women and children are directed to load the lifeboats.

"We Are on the Ice"

y turning sharply to the left, the *Titanic* had avoided a head-on collision with the iceberg. But the starboard side of the ship still struck the ice beneath the water. For approximately ten seconds, the ice ripped at least six long narrow slits in the lower hull, opening approximately 12 square feet (1 sq m) to the ocean. Fleet and Lee watched as the top of the iceberg moved slowly past them. They heard the scraping sound and saw chunks of ice fall onto the deck.

Most passengers were unaware that anything had occurred. Others felt a slight quiver. One passenger said it seemed like the ship had gone over a thousand marbles. Many who were asleep were not awakened.

Jack Thayer was in his room when he felt a slight sway and realized the ship had made a smooth turn. He said that if he had been holding a full glass of water in his hand, not a drop would have spilled. The engines stopped, and everything was disturbingly quiet. Jack heard the noise of running feet and muffled voices in the hallway. He called to his mother and father in the adjoining room to tell them he was "going up on deck to see the fun."[1] His father joined him.

Dressed in pajamas, slippers, and an overcoat, Jack went up to the main deck, where chunks of ice were scattered about. A crew member told Jack and his father that the ship had struck an iceberg. In just 15 minutes, the ship's bow had already started to dip. Although the gashes in the hull were small, the strong water pressure 20 feet (6 m) below the ocean's surface rapidly forced saltwater into the hull.

Some passengers, unaware of the danger, playfully kicked around chunks of ice on the deck. For others, even though the playing cards fell off the table when the ship hit the iceberg, they calmly picked the cards up and dealt another hand. A man in the smoking room lightheartedly suggested that someone go out on deck for some ice to put in his drink. Some passengers headed back to bed after a steward assured them the ship would be steaming toward New York again in two hours.

The Reality

Passengers listened anxiously to alarming reports. When Jack Thayer and his father came in from the cold, they spoke to Ismay, Andrews, and some of the ship's officers. Andrews said the ship did not have much more than an hour. Captain Smith and Andrews had been to the mailroom and squash court; both areas were flooding with water. The fate of this magnificent ship was difficult to believe.

Jack and his father hurried back to their rooms to find Mrs. Thayer and her maid were dressed. Stewards had passed the word that everyone should dress and put on the life preservers that were stored in each room. Jack put on a green tweed suit and a mohair vest. He then added his life preserver made of thick cork and donned his overcoat.

A shout was heard: "All passengers on deck with life belts on."[2] First-class passengers made their way up the Grand Staircase. Some took the time to stop at the purser's office to collect their valuables. In the lower levels, third-class passengers dressed as water crept about their ankles. Many second- and third-class passengers joined those on the deck. Andrews encouraged people to wear their life jackets and board the lifeboats. The first lifeboat to be lowered to the water, number 7, was loaded around midnight. Although it could hold more than 60 passengers, it was less than half full.

A Ship in Distress

When the ship struck the iceberg, Phillips and Bride had been ordered to send CQD signals, the Morse code at that time for a ship in distress. They also used SOS, the new international distress signal.

The Lifeboats

The 16 wooden *Titanic* lifeboats were made of elm and oak. Each boat was supplied with oars, blankets, food, water, and flares. Sails for each boat were stored in painted bags. Each boat had an anchor and a compass. The even-numbered boats hung on the port side; the odd-numbered boats were stored on the starboard side of the ship.

Phillips and Bride frantically sent and received messages nonstop. At 12:25 a.m., their message to the *Carpathia* read, "Come at once. We have struck a berg."[3] At 12:30 a.m., the *Frankfurt* received, "Tell your captain to come to our help. We are on the ice."[4] The *Baltic* assured the *Titanic*, "We are rushing to you."[5] The *Olympic,* 500 miles (805 km) away, fired up its boilers to go full speed to help its sister ship.

At 12:35 a.m., people on the *Titanic* spotted lights of a nearby ship. The crew thought it was the *Californian*. The ship seemed so close that one lifeboat was ordered to row toward it and bring back help. Distress rockets were fired into the sky.

Evacuating the Ship

On A Deck, the lounge was crowded with people. Milton Long had met Jack Thayer at dinner that night. When he saw the Thayers, he asked if he could stay with them. The orchestra played lively tunes, although the worried crowd took little notice.

The crew uncovered lifeboats to swing them over the side of the ship. At times, a deafening noise emitted as engines shut down and boiler steam blew off. The crew loaded and lowered eight lifeboats, but they were afraid to fill the boats to capacity while they were suspended so high above the water. If a boat fell, they reasoned, it might buckle or break.

Jack Thayer lost track of his parents. His mother had boarded a lifeboat, but Jack would never see his father again.

Some people refused to believe the *Titanic* was sinking. Stewards went about their regular duties. The band continued to play. But other passengers understood the *Titanic* was going down. Benjamin Guggenheim and his valet had been watching lifeboats being loaded. Now they returned to their cabins and changed into evening wear. Guggenheim later said, "We've dressed up in our best and are prepared to go down like gentlemen."[6] Major Butt and Francis Millet played a game of cards in the smoking room. Mr. and Mrs. Straus remained in their deck chairs.

In the belly of the ship, crewmen scrambled for their lives. In section 6, the warning bell had rung even before the ship collided with the iceberg. The white light that indicated full speed ahead turned to red, a signal to stop the ship. Firemen shouted to

Together Till the End

Isidor and Ida Straus stood near Lifeboat 8 as it was being loaded. Ida stepped on and then off. She walked over to her husband and said, "We have been living together for many years, and where you go, I go."[7] She gave her fur coat to her maid, who got on the lifeboat. Mr. and Mrs. Straus then walked over to two deck chairs, sat down side by side, and watched quietly.

shut the furnace doors. But before they could shut them all, there was a roaring crash. The ripping of the hull sounded like thunder. Ocean water gushed in through the side of the ship. Section 6 flooded quickly. Stoker Frederick Barrett and fireman George Beauchamp jumped through the doorway to section 5 just as the automatic watertight door was closing. When ordered back to their posts, the men climbed a ladder in an attempt to return to their section. But when they saw that the section was flooded with approximately 8 feet (2 m) of water, they returned to section 5.

Soon a blast of water also engulfed section 5. Barrett climbed up a ladder and then up several staircases until he reached the Promenade Deck. He was put in command of Lifeboat 13, which contained 46 other people. Twenty were men, which was unusual since the order had been given to load women and children first. Five children were on the boat. The youngest, ten-month-old Alden Gates Caldwell, was wrapped tightly in a blanket. The Caldwells were reluctant to get into the lifeboat. They felt it was safer to stay on the ship, which most thought was invincible. But Barrett told them the truth—water was gushing into the ship and the *Titanic* was sinking. Mrs. Caldwell got in with Alden. Her husband Albert stepped in just as the boat was being lowered. The lifeboat was almost to the water's edge when Barrett saw Lifeboat 15 rapidly coming down above them. Barrett and another seaman quickly cut their boat free of its davits, let it drop to the sea, and rowed away.

Twelve-year-old Ruth Becker was also on Lifeboat 13. She later recalled seeing water rushing into the ship while every porthole and lounge still blazed with electric lights.

Lifeboat 15 carried 43 people.

Survivors

Lawrence Beesley wrote about his experience on Lifeboat 13. He mentioned a baby boy who cried continually. Someone realized the baby's feet were exposed. The baby, ten-month-old Alden Gates Caldwell, stopped crying when someone covered up his feet. Caldwell survived the disaster.

Caldwell spoke about what his parents told him of the sinking of the *Titanic*, but the tragedy held little interest for him. In 1986 and 1987, he recorded his recollections of what his parents had told him. These audiotapes are in the archives of the Titanic International Society. Caldwell was invited to a reunion of *Titanic* survivors in 1988 but chose not to attend. He died in 1992 at the age of 81.

Ruth Becker was only 12 when she boarded Lifeboat 13 and was ultimately rescued. In the years after the disaster, Ruth refused to talk about the *Titanic*. When her own children were young, they did not know their mother had been on the fateful maiden voyage of the *Titanic*. However, later in life, she began sharing her harrowing experience. She granted interviews and attended conventions of the Titanic Historical Society. She died in 1990 at the age of 90. Her ashes were scattered over the area where the *Titanic* sank.

Among them were Selma Asplund and two of her five children: five-year-old Lillian and three-year-old Felix. Lillian had been passed through a window of the Promenade Deck and placed in the lifeboat as it was being lowered. Still on the deck, her father held Lillian's twin brother Carl. Her two older brothers were on each side of her father and did not survive.

As the bow of the ship sunk deeper into the water, the wireless operators still frantically sent messages, but their transmissions were now so weak that other ships could barely read them. The last message received by another ship was at 1:45 a.m. It read, "Engine room full up to boilers."[8]

Panicked passengers rushed to the last lifeboats, which were nearly filled to capacity. Fifth Officer Harold Lowe fired his gun when a mob of people attempted to get on Lifeboat 14, which already had 60 people on board. Sadly, most of the lifeboats at sea were less than half full. When the first order came to fill the lifeboats with women and children first, passengers had been reluctant. They believed the ship could not sink and they would have to reboard. Consequently, the first lifeboats left half-empty.

Shortly before 2:00 a.m., John Jacob Astor fought his way to the boat and put his 19-year-old pregnant wife on board. Not allowed to get on, Astor stepped back and waved good-bye to her. The *Titanic* was dipping so far into the ocean that lifeboats had to be lowered only 15 feet (5 m) to reach the water.

The crew now started untying Collapsibles A through D. Ismay managed to get on Collapsible C, even though more than 1,500 people were trying to get on a lifeboat. Second Officer Lightoller ordered the crew to encircle Collapsible D with locked arms so only women and children could board. A "Mr. Louis Hoffman" handed his two little boys through the ring of crewmen, who put his children on the lifeboat. Then he walked away. Hoffman was actually Michel Navratil. He had kidnapped his sons during divorce proceedings and was taking them

The Richest Man on the Ship

As John Astor and his pregnant wife Madeleine waited for a lifeboat, they went to the gymnasium and sat on the mechanical horses. They had life jackets on, but when Astor found a spare one, he cut it open with a knife to show his wife what it was made of. Madeleine boarded Lifeboat 4, but her husband died on the ship.

In August 1912, she gave birth to the couple's son and named him John Jacob Astor after his father. Madeleine inherited $5 million and the use of her late husband's home on Fifth Avenue in New York City as long as she did not remarry. During World War I, Madeleine gave up her husband's fortune and married a successful businessman. The couple divorced in 1933. Madeleine would remarry and divorce once again. She died in 1940 at the age of 47.

The life jacket worn by John Jacob Astor's wife Madeline, who survived by boarding Lifeboat 4.

from France to the United States under assumed names. Navratil would not survive the disaster, but the boys would one day be reunited with their mother and returned to France.

At 2:05 a.m., Captain Smith released the crew from their duties and told them to see to their own safety. Not giving up hope, wireless operator

Phillips, as well as other crew members, continued to send messages. Passengers were now jumping over the side of the ship.

A Roar and an Explosion

Jack Thayer and Milton Long watched from the starboard side as people ran upward, keeping as far away from the railing as possible. A few crewmen struggled to untie the last collapsible lifeboat.

Five minutes later, the bow of the *Titanic* suddenly took a downward lunge. A roar mixed with the explosions and clashes of shattering glass. Thayer remembered:

> the water rushing up toward us was accompanied by a rumbling roar, mixed with more muffled explosions. It was like standing under a steel railway bridge while an express train passes overhead, mingled with the noise of a pressed steel factory and wholesale breakage of china.[9]

Thayer and Long shook hands, wished each other luck, and jumped into the water. Thayer jumped as far out from the ship as he could. Long jumped in closer to the ship. More than likely, Long was pulled into the interior of the ship. Somehow, Thayer made it back up to the surface.

Thayer later recalled:

The rumble and roar continued. Suddenly the whole superstructure of the ship appeared to split … buckle upwards. The second funnel … seemed to be lifted off, emitting a cloud of sparks. It missed me by only twenty or thirty feet. The suction of it drew me down and down, struggling and swimming, practically spent. [10]

Survivors and naval experts scoffed at the young man's story that the ship had split in two as it sank. But it had indeed broken in half. Thayer's story would be confirmed 73 years later. ⌒

The End of a Dream Ship

Thomas Andrews, the managing director of Harland & Wolff, had supervised every detail of the *Titanic*'s construction. He was last seen staring into space in the first-class smoking room. He had removed his life jacket.

Passengers boarding lifeboats

A painting by Henry Reuterdahl based on information from Titanic survivors

RESCUED

At 2:17 a.m., with the bow already on its way to the muddy ocean bottom, the stern rose vertically, dropping hundreds of people into the water. Then the mighty *Titanic* turned, stopped, and stayed in that position. At 2:20 a.m., with barely a ripple, the stern of the most magnificent ship in the world slipped away to its icy Atlantic grave.

Colonel Gracie found himself trapped in a whirlpool that pulled him down into the freezing water. Kicking his way to the surface, he joined Thayer and nearly 30 others on Collapsible B, which had never been turned upright. As the *Titanic* slipped from view, hundreds of survivors floating in the water or sitting in lifeboats uttered a combined sob. A deadly silence followed. Then one by one, people in the icy water began calling for help. Thayer described it as,

> *swelling into … one long continuous wailing chant … gradually dying away, as one after another could no longer withstand the cold and exposure.*[1]

Survivors clinging to Collapsible B recited the Lord's Prayer over and over. None of the partially filled lifeboats returned to rescue people in the water.

Finally, Fifth Officer Lowe transferred some of the people on Lifeboat 14 to other boats and rowed

Helping Out

Wireless operator Harold Bride climbed onto the overturned Collapsible B after the *Titanic* went down. Bride stayed alive throughout the night, but his feet were frozen and crushed. When he was rescued, he climbed up *Carpathia*'s rope ladder with a broken foot. After receiving medical attention, Bride joined the *Carpathia*'s sole wireless operator to send messages and names of survivors to shore.

back to search for survivors. Seaman Joseph Scarrott helped him look. Scarrott later remembered:

> We went in the direction of the cries and came among hundreds
> of dead bodies and lifebelts. We got one man, who died shortly
> after he got into the boat ... There was another man who was
> calling for help, but among the bodies and wreckage it was too
> late for us to reach him ... Cannot say exactly, but think we
> got about twenty off of the Engelhardt boat ("A"). [2]

RENEWED HOPE

Dawn began to break. Almost two hours had passed since the sinking of the *Titanic*. Hundreds lay dead in the water. Survivors could see fields of ice and towering icebergs, some taller than the *Titanic*. And in the distance was a ship—the *Carpathia*. With renewed hope, people took turns rowing toward the vessel that had come to their rescue. A group of men on the bottom of the overturned Collapsible B shouted. There were only 14 of them alive now. Among them were Thayer, Gracie, Lightoller, and Bride. Two lifeboats picked them up and made their way toward the *Carpathia*.

The *Carpathia*'s rope ladders extended to the water. Lifeboats rowed alongside the ship and sent survivors up the ladders one by one. Children were put in sacks and pulled up by a rope. By 8:30 a.m., approximately 700 survivors were on *Carpathia*'s deck, thankful to be alive. Colonel Gracie said, "I ... felt like falling down on my knees and kissing the deck in gratitude for the preservation of my life."[3]

The kindness of the people on the *Carpathia* was overwhelming. They gave the survivors hot food and drink, dry clothing, and medical attention. They wrapped frostbitten feet and hands and set broken bones. During the three-day trip to New York, they listened to people grieve for the loved ones they had lost.

As the *Carpathia* steamed southwesterly toward the United States, the *Mackay-Bennett* steamed southeasterly from Halifax, Nova Scotia. It was the first of four ships hired by the White Star Line to pick up bodies and debris from the sea. It headed to where the *Titanic*

Where Was Captain Smith?

Captain Smith was a veteran of ocean travel. When the *Titanic* collided with the iceberg, he reacted swiftly. Smith ordered an assessment of the damage and its likely effect on the ship. He ordered that the lifeboats be uncovered. After that, however, Smith stopped giving clear orders. Second Officer Lightoller encouraged him to order the loading of the lifeboats. Smith also stayed on the bridge, away from the crew and passengers. Some historians speculate Smith recognized the inevitable fate of the *Titanic* when he learned something he could not truly comprehend: his ship would sink and most of the people on board would die. His inability to act may have contributed to his death.

went down—1,000 miles (1,609 km) due east of Boston and 350 miles (563 km) southeast of Newfoundland, Canada.

The Tragic News Spreads

The White Star Line offices in New York and London were mobbed by frantic relatives and friends looking for news of loved ones who had been on the fateful voyage. On Thursday evening, April 18, 1912, the *Carpathia* arrived in New York. Its first stop was the White Star Line pier, where crew members deposited the *Titanic*'s empty

Buried at Sea

White Star Line hired the *Mackay-Bennett* to recover the bodies. When it reached the site of the wreck on April 21, 1912, there were many more bodies floating in the water than expected. After seven days of searching, the *Mackay-Bennett* recovered 306 bodies. Of these, 116 bodies were buried at sea, but only 56 of those were identified. Captain Lardner justified his actions:

No prominent man was recommitted to the deep. ... Most of those who were buried out there were members of the *Titanic*'s crew. The man who lives by the sea ought to be satisfied to be buried at sea. I think it is the best place. For my own part I should be contented to be committed to the deep.[4]

The ship returned to its home port at Halifax, Nova Scotia, Canada, the morning of April 30, 1912. Among the 60 bodies that were still unidentified were five women and a baby girl. The rest were believed to be crew members. The first body claimed was that of John Jacob Astor. An "accidental drowning" death certificate was issued. His body was turned over to his son Vincent. The second body claimed was that of Isidor Straus.

lifeboats. When the ship docked at the Cunard Line berth, a crowd of reporters and relatives swarmed the dock in hope of finding out what had happened and who had survived. Some survivors told reporters what they knew. Others were taken immediately to hospitals. A few found friends or family among the crowd. And many would not talk about the disaster.

LOOKING FOR ANSWERS

The next morning, Friday, April 19, the U.S. Senate began its inquiry. The U.S. Navy had intercepted messages that Ismay planned to return to Britain without setting foot on American soil. The U.S. government could not force him to testify if he was not in the United States. Ismay was subpoenaed and required to appear at the inquiry.

The first witness before the Senate Committee on Friday morning—J. Bruce Ismay—arrived under bodyguard protection. Ironically, the hearings were held at the Waldorf-Astoria Hotel—the hotel complex that John Jacob Astor and his cousin William Waldorf had built.

On April 25, after intense questioning by the U.S. Senate Committee, Ismay's written request to return to Britain was denied. Meanwhile, England's

Board of Trade began its own investigation—the British Wreck Commissioner's Inquiry. Both countries called numerous people to testify in an attempt to determine what caused the *Titanic* to sink. Was it poor ship construction? The absence of binoculars? A shortage of lifeboats? Was the ship going too fast for the conditions? Who was to blame—Ismay? Captain Smith? The two lookouts? The White Star Line? Could everyone have been saved if the nearby *Californian* had responded to the *Titanic*'s distress calls and flares?

Both investigations determined that the loss of the *Titanic* was "due to collision with an iceberg, brought about by the excessive speed at which the ship was being navigated."[5] It was found that Captain Smith was not at fault, although he made a grievous mistake by not decreasing the ship's speed or assigning extra lookouts. Both inquiries laid much of the blame for the loss of life on the crew and the captain of the *Californian* for not responding to the *Titanic*'s distress signals.

A Coward and a Villain

Newspapers portrayed Ismay as a scoundrel for ignoring iceberg warnings and forcing Captain Smith to push the ship to its limits of speed. He was depicted in cartoons as a villain who deserted his ship to save himself while women and children were still on board. British society would shun him and label him a coward for the rest of his life.

The April 15, 1912, issue of the New York Times *reported the sinking of the* Titanic.

Approximate location of *Titanic*

April 14, 1912
1:55 p.m.

United Kingdom

Ireland

France

New York

Titanic

Carpathia

ATLANTIC

The Titanic's route

A SUNLESS ABYSS

ithin five days of the sinking of the
Titanic, people made plans to find
the wreck. Vincent Astor, son of millionaire John
Jacob Astor, wanted to locate the ship, blow up the
hull, and recover his father's body when it floated to

the surface. But his plan was abandoned when the *Mackay-Bennett* retrieved Astor's body from the water.

That same year, the Astor, Widener, and Guggenheim families hired a wrecking company to find and raise the *Titanic*. But the company did not have the necessary equipment to access such a deep, dangerous spot. The following year, an architect planned to find the ship by attaching electromagnets to a submarine. He believed the magnets would draw the submarine to the *Titanic*'s metal hull. This plan, as well as others, was dropped, and interest in finding the wreck subsided, especially during World War I.

REMEMBERING THE TRAGEDY

Some survivors wrote down what they remembered about that terrible night at sea. Others compiled what passengers had said and what newspapers had reported. Colonel Archibald Gracie finished his book, *The Truth About the* Titanic, shortly before his death on December 4, 1912—less than eight months after the ship sank. It was published in 1913.

Learning from Disaster

American and British investigations into the sinking of the *Titanic* led to laws that made ocean travel safer. The International Ice Patrol was formed in 1914 to monitor and publicize the location of icebergs. All ships had to have enough lifeboats to seat everyone on board. Passenger ships had to have radio operators on duty around the clock.

Lawrence Beesley also wrote a book, *The Loss of the S.S. Titanic by One of the Survivors*, which was published in 1912. Arthur Rostron, captain of the *Carpathia*, wrote *Home from the Sea* in 1931. Second Officer Lightoller also wrote his story, *Titanic and Other Ships*, in 1935. In 1940, at the age of 45, Jack Thayer wrote his experiences as a 17-year-old passenger. His pamphlet was called *The Sinking of the S.S. Titanic*.

New Technology and an Obsession

More than 40 years had passed since the *Titanic*'s maiden voyage. Yet explorers were still attempting to find the ocean liner in its sunless abyss. In 1953, British salvage company Risdon Beasley quietly and unsuccessfully hunted for the sunken ship. In 1981, Jack Grimm led a team using underwater sonar equipment to find the *Titanic*. They missed the ship by 1.5 miles (2.4 km).

Finding the *Titanic*'s grave became the obsession of many throughout the world. Most of the search schemes were impossible; others were extremely costly. Some people imagined the ship undamaged and resting in its original magnificence on the ocean floor. Others believed the ship contained jewels and gold. Most searches were deterred by the rough seas of the Atlantic. All were confused by its true location and conflicting reports about where the *Titanic* went down. By the mid-1980s, millions of dollars had been spent on failed attempts to find the ship of dreams.

In 1985, more than seven decades after the sinking, the *Titanic* was discovered. Scientist Robert D. Ballard had followed Grimm's expeditions closely and believed Grimm had not spent enough time looking for the ship. Because the *Titanic* had gone down in such deep water, special search equipment was designed to withstand the immense pressure. Ballard developed a deep-sea video camera sled that could be lowered from the surface and towed over the ocean floor. It fed live video images to the surface through a fiber-optic leash. The U.S. Navy agreed to fund a three-week search for the *Titanic* including a test of this unmanned deep-sea vessel, named *Argo*. By the summer of 1985, Ballard prepared to go to sea as part of a joint French-American expedition to seek the remains of the *Titanic*.

Since the exact location of the *Titanic* was unclear, Ballard's strategy was to search a large rectangular area of the ocean. On August 24, 1985, Ballard and his team of researchers arrived somewhere above the *Titanic* aboard the research vessel *Knorr*. The *Argo* was sent down and controlled remotely, going back and forth in a grid pattern that Ballard likened to mowing the lawn. Amidst technical problems, the *Argo* was recording only sand and mud after six days. On September 1, 1985, a huge round structure appeared on *Knorr*'s video monitors. It was one of the *Titanic*'s huge boilers.

Knowing that the rest of the ship had to be near, the team kept searching. Finally, the *Argo* passed over the main hull of the *Titanic*. For six minutes, the *Knorr* crew observed on video screen the upright bow of the ship in nearly 13,000 feet (3,962 m) of water and 60 feet (18 m) of mud. The crew cheered and clapped but then fell silent in reverence for those who had lost their lives. On September 9, 1985, exhausted and drained, Ballard told a press conference:

> The Titanic *lies in 13,000 feet of water … overlooking a small canyon … upright on the bottom. There is no light at this great depth and little life can be found. It is a quiet and peaceful and fitting place for the remains of this greatest of sea tragedies to rest. May it forever remain that way and may God bless these found souls.* [1]

Ballard recommended to Congress that the *Titanic* remain undisturbed and that artifacts be recovered and protected.

In 1986, Ballard set out again with a manned deep-sea submersible named *Alvin* and its small, remotely controlled deep-sea camera pod named *Jason Jr.* or *J.J.* When the *Alvin* crew reached the wreckage on 11 dives, they explored and took photographs. They also released the powerful robot *J.J.* on three of the dives. *J.J.* entered *Titanic*'s broken glass dome at the top of the Grand Staircase. Once

Watertight and Unsinkable?

The *Titanic* had 15 solid walls, or "bulkheads," connecting the port and starboard sides of the lower decks. Because the top of the bulkheads extended approximately 15 feet (4.5 m) above the waterline, the White Star Line boasted that the compartments were watertight, making the ship virtually unsinkable. The *Titanic* was built to float if any two compartments took on water. It could even float if the first four compartments in the bow were opened to the sea. And that might have been true if the *Titanic* had not had an unusual crash.

When the *Titanic* collided with the iceberg, it opened the first five compartments. The water poured in, adding weight that pulled the bow down, allowing the water rushing in to rise higher against the bulkheads. Eventually, the water pushed the *Titanic* low enough to allow spillage over the "watertight" walls. The bulkheads had not been sealed at the top, which would have prevented the overflow. Water flowed from the fifth compartment to the sixth, from one compartment to the next until the *Titanic* could take no more. The process was somewhat similar to filling an ice cube tray by tilting it and putting one end under a faucet —the water flows from one section to another.

Thomas Andrews recognized the problem within minutes and told Captain Smith the *Titanic* would sink. Nothing could prevent it.

inside the ship, the robot moved down several decks, taking pictures of crystal chandeliers that were still intact. *J.J.* moved into rooms and crevices, filming places where people had once slept, ate, read, and died. It photographed areas that appeared untouched as well as sections that had been devastated. It recorded what time, water, and microorganisms had done to deteriorate what once was a magnificent vessel.

On this voyage, the team also found the stern. It lay approximately a half mile (.8 km) south of the bow. Between the two parts of the ship, unbroken china cups, a bathtub, the ceramic head of a doll, a silver bowl, and thousands of leather shoes had been strewn across the ocean floor.

The stern had rotated, and in its descent, with hundreds of people climbing up its slanted deck, had taken a violent plunge. Air pockets that remained trapped inside were squeezed by the pressure of the water. As its steel plates twisted and crumpled, the structure finally imploded. When the stern of the *Titanic* struck the bottom at full speed, it nearly flattened on impact and the rush of water peeled back its hull like a can opener.

Ballard wrote, "The decks themselves sandwiched upon each other, pressing ceilings and floors together as if the stern contorted to match the human agony."[2] Ballard made voyages to the *Titanic* in 1985, 1986, and 2004. On his final voyage, he left a plaque on the stern:

> In memory of those souls who perished with the 'Titanic,' April 14–15, 1912.[3]

Ballard's exploration teams brought back remarkable videotapes and photographs of the *Titanic*. Ballard asked Congress to declare the *Titanic* an international memorial. He considered it "hallowed ground" and believed the world should protect the ship like other national and international treasures.

Although Ballard thought the discovery of the *Titanic* would satisfy people's curiosities, it did just the opposite. It relit the fire of fascination with the sunken ship. Expeditions by others have provided more photographs and recovered *Titanic* artifacts.

Brittle Steel

In 1996, more than 200 pounds (91 kg) of steel from the *Titanic* were brought to the surface. Samples were tested. By today's standards, scientists found that the steel was full of imperfections that created weak areas. This caused the steel to be brittle. Under extreme temperature conditions, such as below-freezing water, the steel would be fragile.

On the night of the disaster, the steel was exposed to cold temperatures and unusual stress from striking the iceberg. Scientists now believe the hull may have shattered like glass, allowing ocean water to gush in and finally causing the ship to break in half.

Ravaged by Time

At the bottom of the Atlantic Ocean, sea organisms eat away at what remains of the *Titanic*. Ultimately, this may cause the fragile ship to collapse and turn to dust on the ocean floor. Even after the ship is gone, the stories of those who perished and those who survived will live on. They will be memorialized in artifacts, books, movies, and museums. But above all, people will remember this ship of dreams that surpassed every vessel of its time. And the world will also remember the lives that were changed forever in some way by the tragedy of the *Titanic*. ⌐

Pipes and the bathtub in what was once Captain Smith's cabin

TIMELINE

1912

The *Titanic* completes its sea trials. On April 2, it departs Belfast, Ireland, for Southampton, England.

1912

The *Titanic* departs from Southampton on April 10 at 12:15 p.m. and nearly collides with the *New York*.

1912

Approximately five hours later, the *Titanic* arrives at Cherbourg, France.

1912

Wireless system breaks down at 11:00 p.m. on April 13. It is out of order for six hours.

1912

The *Titanic* receives multiple reports of ice fields on the morning of April 14.

1912

The *Titanic* scrapes an iceberg on its starboard side on April 14 at 11:40 p.m.

1912	1912	1912
The *Titanic* drops anchor at Queenstown, Ireland, on April 11 around noon.	The *Titanic* departs for New York City on April 11 at 1:30 p.m.	The *Titanic* receives warning about a thick ice field at 7:00 p.m. on April 12.

1912	1912	1912
On April 15, the *Titanic* sends its first distress message at 12:15 a.m.	The first lifeboat is launched at 12:45 a.m.	The *Titanic* sinks at 2:20 a.m.

TIMELINE

1912

On April 15, at 4:10 a.m., the *Carpathia* arrives to rescue survivors.

1912

The *Carpathia* arrives in New York on April 18.

1912

U.S. Senate Inquiry begins on April 19; J. Bruce Ismay is the first witness.

1953

Salvage firm Risdon Beasley unsuccessfully searches for the *Titanic*.

1985

On September 1, an expedition led by Dr. Robert Ballard discovers the bow of the *Titanic*.

1986

Dr. Ballard's team discovers the stern of the *Titanic*.

1912

Mackay-Bennett arrives at the site of the sinking on April 21 to retrieve bodies.

1931

Carpathia's Captain Rostron publishes *Home from the Sea.*

1935

Second Officer Lightoller writes Titanic *and Other Ships.*

2004

Dr. Ballard's team leaves a memorial plaque at the stern of the *Titanic.*

Essential Facts

Date of Event

April 10, 1912, to April 15, 1912

Place of Event

- Belfast, Ireland: the *Titanic* was built in a specially constructed dry dock
- Southampton, England: crew and passengers boarded the *Titanic*
- Cherbourg, France: final passengers boarded the *Titanic*
- Queenstown, Ireland: additional passengers boarded the *Titanic*
- Atlantic Ocean

Key Players

- J. Bruce Ismay, managing director of the White Star Line
- Captain Edward John Smith
- Wireless operators Jack Phillips and Harold Bride
- Passengers and crew members
- *Carpathia*

Highlights of Event

❖ The White Star Line built the *Titanic* to be the largest, most luxurious, and fastest passenger ship.

❖ The number of lifeboats on the ship were reduced because they blocked the ocean view. There were not enough lifeboats for all passengers and crew in an emergency.

❖ Captain Smith ignored early warnings from the *La Touraine* and other ships of a thick field of ice.

❖ Despite many ice warnings, Captain Smith ordered that the *Titanic*'s speed be increased.

❖ Captain Smith cancelled the scheduled lifeboat drill.

❖ An iceberg warning from the U.S. Navy never made it out of the *Titanic*'s wireless room.

❖ The *Titanic* struck an iceberg and a wireless message was sent asking for assistance.

❖ Initially, passengers were not aware of the danger and the possibility that the ship would sink. Many did not board lifeboats.

❖ Approximately two hours after the *Titanic* sank, the *Carpathia* arrived to help rescue people.

Quote

"It seemed almost as if she might clear it, but I suppose there was ice under water … It was a dark mass that came through that haze and there was no white appearing until it was just close alongside the ship, and that was just a fringe at the top … As she struck … there was a certain amount of ice that came on board the ship."
—*Reginald Lee*, Lookout on the *Titanic*

ADDITIONAL RESOURCES

SELECT BIBLIOGRAPHY

Ballard, Robert D. *The Discovery of the* Titanic, Toronto: Warner/Madison, 1987.

Ballard, Robert D. *Return to* Titanic: *A New Look at the World's Most Famous Lost Ship*. Washington, D.C.: National Geographic, 2004.

Beesley, Lawrence, Archibald Gracie, Commander Lightoller, and Harold Bride. Ed. Jack Winocour. *The Story of the* Titanic *as Told by Its Survivors*. Mineola, NY: Dover Publications, 1960.

Butler, Daniel Allen. *"Unsinkable": The Full Story of the RMS* Titanic. Mechanicsburg, PA: Stackpole Books, 1998.

Eaton, John P., and Charles A. Haas. Titanic: *Triumph and Tragedy*. New York: W.W. Norton & Company, 1995.

Green, Rod. *Building the* Titanic: *An Epic Tale of the Creation of History's Most Famous Ocean Liner*. Pleasantville, NY: The Reader's Digest Association, 2005.

Mowbray, Jay Henry, ed. *Sinking of the* Titanic: *Eyewitness Accounts*. Mineola, NY: Dover Publications, 1998.

Quinn, Paul J. Titanic *at Two A.M.: An Illustrated Narrative with Survivor Accounts*. Saco, ME: Fantail, 1997.

FURTHER READING

Aaseng, Nathan. *The* Titanic. San Diego, CA: Lucent Books, 1999.

Adams, Simon. Titanic. New York: DK Publishing, 1999.

Conklin, Thomas. *The* Titanic *Sinks*. New York: Random House, 1997.

Molony, Senan. Titanic: *A Primary Source History*. Milwaukee, WI: Gareth Stevens Publishing, 2006.

Sherrow, Victoria. *The* Titanic. San Diego, CA: Lucent Books, 1999.

Web Links

To learn more about the *Titanic*, visit ABDO Publishing Company on the World Wide Web at **www.abdopublishing.com**. Web sites about the *Titanic* are featured on our Book Links page. These links are routinely monitored and updated to provide the most current information available.

Places To Visit

Maritime Museum of the Atlantic
1675 Lower Water Street, Halifax, Nova Scotia, Canada B3J 1S3
902-424-7490
http://museum.gov.ns.ca/mma
The *Titanic* exhibit includes artifacts that were found while Halifax crews searched for victims.

The Titanic Historical Society Museum
208 Main Street, Indian Orchard, MA 01151-0053
413-543-4770
http://www.titanichistoricalsociety.org/museum
The museum houses a collection of rare *Titanic* survivor artifacts, many donated by survivors, including the life jacket of Mrs. John Jacob Astor. Stories of the passengers and crew members are represented.

Glossary

abyss
A deep space.

aft
Near, toward, or at the stern of a ship.

berth
A single bed in a shared room.

boat train
A train that regularly carries people from a city to a port.

bow
The forward part of a ship.

bridge
A raised area at the front of the ship that provides a clear view for the navigation of the ship.

CQD
An early Morse code distress signal.

crow's nest
A partly enclosed platform on a ship's mast for use as a lookout.

davit
Cranelike device that holds and lowers lifeboats.

dry dock
A dock that can be kept dry for use during the construction or repairing of ships.

gangway
A ramp used to enter or exit a ship.

hull
The frame of a ship.

invincible
Incapable of being destroyed.

maritime
> Of, or pertaining to, the sea.

omen
> A sign of something about to happen.

port
> The side of a ship that is on the left when a person faces forward.

promenade
> A walkway.

ragtime
> A style of jazz.

sea trial
> A ship's trial runs to determine its readiness as a fully operational ship.

squash
> An indoor racquet sport named after the "squashable" soft ball used in the game.

starboard
> The side of a ship that is on the right when a person faces forward.

stern
> The rear of a ship.

subpoenaed
> Given a legal order to appear to give testimony.

tenders
> Boats that help other ships with communication or transport people and supplies between shore and a larger ship.

wireless
> An early form of radio communication.

SOURCE NOTES

Chapter 1. Voices of the Atlantic
1. John B. Thayer. *The Sinking of the S.S.* Titanic. Chicago: Academy Chicago Publishers, 1998. 349.
2. Archibald Gracie. *The Truth About the* Titanic. New York: Mitchell Kennerley, 1913. 89.
3. "Mr. Charles John Joughin." *Encyclopedia Titanica.* 28 Jan. 2007 <http://www.encyclopedia-titanica.org/biography.php?id=1945>.

Chapter 2. The Making of a Giant
1. "95 Years Ago: The Forgotten Maiden Voyage." 22 Aug. 2007 <http://www.titanicfiles.org/Essays_englisch/Olympic%20Maiden%20Voyage.pdf>.
2. Susan Wels. Titanic: *Legacy of the World's Greatest Ocean Liner.* New York: Time Life Books, 1997. 44.

Chapter 3. Maiden Voyage
1. Lawrence Beesley. *The Loss of the S.S.* Titanic. Boston: Houghton Mifflin Company, 2000. 8–9.
2. "Mr. Percy Andrew Bailey." *Encyclopedia Titanica.* 17 Feb. 2007 <http://www.encyclopedia-titanica.org/biography/333/>.
3. Susan Wels. Titanic: *Legacy of the World's Greatest Ocean Liner.* New York: Time Life Books, 1997. 49–52.
4. Senan Molony. Titanic: *A Primary Source History.* Milwaukee, WI: Gareth Stevens Publishing, 2006. 15.

Chapter 4. Four Days of Extravagance
None.

Chapter 5. Fields of Ice
1. Lawrence Beesley. *The Loss of the S.S.* Titanic. Boston: Houghton Mifflin Company; 2000. 21.
2. Archibald Gracie. *The Truth About the* Titanic. New York: Mitchell Kennerley, 1913. 2.

Chapter 6. "Iceberg Right Ahead"
1. Archibald Gracie. *The Truth About the* Titanic. New York: Mitchell Kennerley, 1913. 5.
2. "Eternal Father, Strong to Save: The Navy Hymn." *Naval Historical Center.* Department of the Navy. 22 Aug. 2007 <http://www.navy.mil/navydata/questions/eternal.html>.
3. Susan Wels. Titanic: *Legacy of the World's Greatest Ocean Liner.* New York: Time Life Books, 1997. 80.
4. John B. Thayer. *The Sinking of the S.S.* Titanic. Chicago: Academy Chicago Publishers, 1998. 334.
5. Susan Wels. Titanic: *Legacy of the World's Greatest Ocean Liner.* New York: Time Life Books, 1997. 80.
6. Walter Lord. *A Night to Remember*. New York: Bantam Books, 1997. 28.
7. Susan Wels. Titanic: *Legacy of the World's Greatest Ocean Liner.* New York: Time Life Books, 1997. 83.
8. Ibid. 84.
9. "British Wreck Commissioner's Inquiry: Day 4." Titanic *Inquiry Project: Electronic Copies of the Inquiries into the Disaster.* TitanicInquiry.org. 10 Mar. 2007 <http://www.titanicinquiry.org/BOTInq/BOTInq04Lee01.php>.
10. Ibid.
11. Senan Molony. "*Birma*'s Wireless Bears Witness!" *Encyclopedia Titanica.* 10 Mar. 2007 <http://www.encyclopedia-titanica.org/item/5395/>.

Source Notes Continued

Chapter 7. "We Are on the Ice"

1. Jack Thayer. *The Sinking of the S.S.* Titanic. Chicago: Academy Chicago Publishers, 1998. 336.
2. Susan Wels. Titanic: *Legacy of the World's Greatest Ocean Liner.* New York: Time Life Books, 1997. 88.
3. *"Titanic* Wireless Distress Messages Sent and Received April 14–15, 1912." *Great Ships.* 16 Mar. 2007 <http://web.greatships. net:81/distress.html>.
4. Ibid.
5. Ibid.
6. "Mr. Benjamin Guggenheim." *Encyclopedia Titanica.* 24 Feb. 2007 <http://www.encyclopedia-titanica.org/biography/143/>.
7. "United States Senate Inquiry: Testimony of Alfred Crawford." Titanic *Inquiry Project: Electronic Copies of the Inquiries into the Disaster.* 24 Feb. 2007 <http://www.titanicinquiry.org/USInq/ AmInq01Crawford01.php>.
8. *"Titanic* Wireless Distress Messages Sent and Received April 14–15, 1912." *Great Ships.* 16 Mar. 2007 <http://web.greatships. net:81/distress.html>.
9. John B. Thayer. *The Sinking of the S.S.* Titanic. Chicago: Academy Chicago Publishers, 1998. 344.
10. Ibid. 346.

Chapter 8. Rescued
1. John B. Thayer. *The Sinking of the S.S.* Titanic. Chicago: Academy Chicago Publishers, 1998. 348–349.
2. "Mr. Joseph George Scarrott." *Encyclopedia Titanica.* 24 Feb. 2007 <http://www.encyclopedia-titanica.org/biography/1372>.
3. Archibald Gracie. *The Truth About the* Titanic. New York: Mitchell Kennerley, 1913. 111.
4. Jay Henry Mowbray. *Sinking of the* Titanic: *Eyewitness Accounts.* Mineola, N.Y.: Dover Publications, 1998. 261–262.
5. "British Wreck Commissioner's Inquiry Report on the Loss of the *Titanic*." Titanic *Inquiry Project: Electronic Copies of the Inquiries into the Disaster.* 28 Feb. 2007 <http://www.titanicinquiry.org/BOTInq/ BOTReport/BOTRep01.php>.

Chapter 9. A Sunless Abyss
1. Daniel Allen Butler. *"Unsinkable": The Full Story of the RMS* Titanic. Cambridge, MA: Da Capo, 2002. 214.
2. Robert D. Ballard. *Return to* Titanic: *A New Look at the World's Most Famous Lost Ship.* Washington, D.C.: National Geographic, 2004. 13.
3. Ibid. 17.

INDEX

ABOUT THE AUTHOR

Sue Vander Hook has been writing and editing books for more than 15 years. Although her writing career began with several nonfiction books for adults, her main focus is educational books for children and young adults. She especially enjoys writing about historical events and biographies of people who made a difference. Her published works also include a high school curriculum and several series on disease, technology, and sports. Sue lives with her family in Minnesota.

PHOTO CREDITS

AP Images, cover, 3, 20, 96 (top); Bettmann/Corbis, 6, 46, 51, 52, 61, 64, 77, 85, 96 (bottom), 98; Max Dannenbaum/Getty Images, 11, 97 (bottom); Ralph White/Corbis, 12, 26; Hulton-Deutsch Collection/Corbis, 19; Pat Sullivan/AP Images, 31; Corbis, 33; The Mariners' Museum/Corbis, 34; Underwood & Underwood/Corbis, 41, 43; Eric Risberg/AP Images, 45, 97 (top); Time Life Pictures/Mansell/Getty Images, 63, 78; Nancy Palmieri/AP Images, 74; National Ocean and Atmospheric Administration/AP Images, 95, 99